Winter Walk:

A Collection of Poems

Brian Wood

SAKURA PUBLISHING
Hermitage, Pennsylvania
USA

Winter Walk:

A Collection of Poems

Brian Wood

Winter Walk: A Collection of Poems
Copyright © 2013 by Brian Wood

All rights reserved. Published in the United States by Sakura Publishing in 2013. No part of this publication may be reproduced, distributed, or transmitted in any form or by any means, including photocopying, recording, or other electronic or mechanical methods, without the prior written permission of the publisher, except in the case of brief quotations embodied in critical reviews and certain other noncommercial uses permitted by copyright law. For permission requests, write to the publisher, addressed "Attention: Permissions Coordinator," at the address below.

Sakura Publishing
PO BOX 1681
Hermitage, PA 16148

www.sakura-publishing.com

Ordering Information:

Quantity sales. Special discounts are available on quantity purchases by corporations, associations, and others. For details, contact the publisher at the address above. Orders by U.S. trade bookstores and wholesalers. Please contact Sakura Publishing: Tel: (330) 360-5131; or visit www.sakura-publishing.com.

Book Cover and Design by Rania Meng
Book Interior Editing and Design by Peter Santilli
Author Photo by Rachel Sentes
Cigar in Author Photo Courtesy of Tim Micallef

First Edition
Printed in the United States of America
ISBN-10:0988962837
ISBN-13:978-0-9889628-3-5
14 13 12 11 10 / 10 9 8 7 6 5 4 3 2 1

"Brian Wood is the kind of poet who reminds me of my favorites (Larkin, Frost, Auden). His poems have a meter, and form, and a classicism that is missing from most modern poetry. His words have a refreshing resonance that reaches far beyond what you see on the page. I enjoy them a great deal."

--Thomas Trofimuk, author of *Waiting For Columbus*

"Any man who loves dogs and words, especially together, is someone I like. Anyone who uses those words as Brian Wood does in this collection of his poems, I admire. There are questions here, some with answers, all provoking. There are moments here we have all felt, both of helplessness and of surprising inner strength. Take a walk with his dogs and his words -- you'll find it refreshing."

--Roy MacGregor, author of *Northern Light*

ACKNOWLEGDEMENTS

Derek Vasconi; Sergeant Michael McGuire, U.S. Army; Doug and Kim Stringer; Paul and Julie Gendron; Mary-Louise and Glenn Marcus; Nicole Langlois; my parents; Sophie Dikeakos; Bob McKenzie; Al Strachan; James Duthie; Allan Walsh; my brother; Roy MacGregor; Thomas Trofimuk; Jared Bland; Michael Holmes; Peter Midgley; Brad Wilson; Silas White; Noelle Allan; Wayne Clifford; David Lyle Jeffrey; Captain Preston Pysh, U.S. Army; Amanda Stevens; Andrew Steeves; John Anonby; Tom Groves; Rick Broadhead; Robert Mackwood; Peter Santilli.

CONTENTS

And Can It Be, 1
July 4, 5
Undercover Boss, 9
Letter to Amy Adams, 11
North Mission Road, 17
Winter Walk, 21
Across Burrard Inlet, 25
Rapture, 27
Giants Game I, 33
Giants Game II, 37
Tips on Immortality (At Venice Beach), 39
Out For a Walk After Dinner, 41
Tongues on Fire, 43
Tuesday, 47
Valentine's Day, 51
El Perrero, 53
The Natural Noise of Good, 57
Pied Beauty, 59
Infatuwhatnow?, 61
Star Flyer, 65
Heaven, 67
Clear Glass, 69
Christmas Lights, 73
The Old Rugged Cross, 77
November 7, 2008, 81
Perfection on Earth, 87
At Flyball, 89
Snow At Night, 95
Nicole On Vacation, 97
Night Storm, 99
Thought Experiments, 101

Sing-Along-Messiah, 105
Ambleside, 109
English Bay, 111
Whose Heart Is Conquered, 113
Joy Unspeakable, 117
Poetry in Transit, 119

About the Author, 123

DEDICATION

For Rachel,
ogni altra cosa, ogni pensier va fore, /
e sol ivi con voi rimansi amore.

PREFACE

The first thing you will notice about these poems is that, with a few exceptions, they are classical in style; that is, they rhyme or scan, sometimes both. Most modern poetry (even the very best) does neither. This is to its detriment, and if this collection has an artistic purpose, it is to be atavistic: to remind us that poems used to follow rules and were the better for it. To me (and to millions of others) Shakespeare is all the more impressive because his greatest work either rhymes or scans or both. The rare exceptions, the poets who can flout rules, like e.e. cummings, should stay that way: exceptions. I am not about to deny his talent. But poetry since him has devolved into everyone doing free verse, all the time. It is just like modern music since Schoenberg: I am not about to deny his talent either, but who looks forward to new classical music? The rare exceptions, such as Pärt, stay that way: exceptions. Otherwise, when you go to classical music concerts that feature music written after 1960, you can literally hear the audience get bored, restless, and finally insulted.

I have seen people walk out. No doubt you have too.

Why? Because Schoenberg and his disciples ignore the general public. To appreciate atonal or dissonant composing, you have to study music for years. Most of us do not have the luxury or the formal trained ear, and whatever elegance there may be in (say) the *Phantasy for Violin and Piano* is quite lost to us.

You can't help but notice that popular poetry, whether it be the kind we find in greeting cards, pop music, hip hop, or anything else people pay actual money for, always rhymes or scans, usually both.

A friend of mine once sent me a series of comments, a lot of them very highly critical, on a draft of a poem I was working on. She broke off to say—

> *"This is a line that could fit right into a Hopkins poem from centuries ago (and that is a GOOD thing. I miss the elegance of poems like his)."*

I get a lot of comments like this, even from people who don't much care for my stuff, not because I am as good as Hopkins, but because they miss poetry that follows rules, and expresses itself formally even when it looks informal. Hopkins sometimes seems bizarre, unidiomatic, even anarchic, but there isn't a syllable out of place. And to me, Larkin is all the more remarkable because his poems look informal, when they are anything but.

The last poem in the collection is the last one because I want to say something about poetry itself. The modern poetry I read is often very, very good. Even the "Poetry In Transit" ones I make fun of. But it makes no attempt to rhyme or scan and seems to me an inferior form of a difficult art. I know I am not alone--what contemporary poet has the stature of Tennyson? Betjeman? Eliot? No name comes to mind, because contemporary poetry has, mostly, ignored the general reader.

If I have an artistic ambition, it is to remind people of poets like Frost, Auden, Yeats, and Milton. I am not saying the poems are anywhere near as good. I am saying they are a deliberate step away from contemporary poetry and a glance back to when rhyme enhanced a beautiful language, and when meter tempered a wild tongue, making it gleam all the more brightly.

                                      Brian Wood

AND CAN IT BE

By the Rideau river, on this lazy,
Still Sunday evening, cars either drive by
Swiftly, or slowly turn in here at the
Mall parking lot, coming in twos and threes.
You'd think they were going to the movies,
But no, all the cars facing a make-do
Stage have their windows wide open for church:
It's drive-in night for Bethel Pentecostal.

Although it might seem odd, it is much like
The service in the morning; members, and
Any passing adherent, would know the
Liturgy. A short prayer, followed by
Two of Wesley's Greatest Hits, then that day's
Bulletin, then another hymn, then a
Sermon, the speaker's words echoing off
The mall storefronts, and mixing with drive-thru

Orders at the burger place. And when he
Has wished perfect peace, the cars line up to
Leave by the one marked exit, some dropping
Bills into big KFC buckets, and
Some joking that they 'gave at the office.'
As the cars meander out, in no real
Rush, by a now sound-asleep river, you
Wonder if these clear pictures in your mind

Will seem like a relic, a romance, some
Thing no longer true, like a flat earth. Will
Scholars have to painfully (step-by-step)
Reconstruct this for their bored students? In
An eon, will the man who goes to church
Appear quaint, as the savage, angry at
The rain god, seems to us? Or will they check
That smirk, and notice the single burning

Drive pushing the poet, artist and the
Cars in their neat rows, to be around for
The birth and death of any tree, to run
With rivers, to keep eyes always open,
And above all, to be something present,
Never in the past or forgotten? And
No setting sun behind oceans would mean
A premonition for us, since Eden

Could move from the beginning of the world
To being here, now and tomorrow, a
Garden for people truly free. They would
Soar as high as those lazy, bored crows did,
In and out of the shadows of the mall
Parking lot, seemingly indifferent
To tonight's text--the future of love, and
A hushed peace, passing all understanding.

August 2012

JULY 4

I am from St Louis. I am forty years old.
I have served over eighteen years, and in this cursed
Country more than five, and yet I'll stay with the plan
Until the President says so. I am now first
Sergeant; two hundred troops say "Sir" to me, all told;
It is July 4, at Camp Spann, Afghanistan.

And what could be a headline to you is, for me,
Routine. It's our job to keep the streets and roads clean;
Each day we look for IEDs that bitter hate
Has left, bombs designed to kill or maim; I have seen
Them do both. So far in this war the enemy
Has taken too many of my men. That makes for late

Nights; I can't believe they are actually gone.
I am not making light of your problems, but try
Taking one of your own soldiers, killed in combat,
To the closest hospital. You keep asking 'Why?'
And your questions have no end. I am always on
Those roads. I wake and think "It's my fault, I feel that,

I know that." In my fevered imagination,
They'd be showing up for a Fourth of July feast
Right about now. But someone filled with hate got to
Them, and I could not stop it. I recall the least
Little thing; the memories play in my head in
A loop, like a bad film always on late, that you

Never liked anyway, but is on all the time:
There is no price I would not pay for even one
Life back, or a slight easing of death's iron grip,
Some relief for their families. And me. The run
Ends here; I don't want (ever) my child on this climb
Up the steepest slope, where you look for that last trip

Home; for this is not home; and this mission cannot
Last forever. They must free their own land. As for
That, it will cost lives; old roots are sown here, and real
Freedom rare. And the younger soldiers who want more
Action--I tell them, that war has a simple plot--
The enemy dies--or you. Those who want blood steel

Your heart. For me, though, I must serve, follow this star.
This does not please everyone. My friends back home say
"Why? Think of all the indifferent ones who will
Not even vote!" Yet I do, so that others may.
How impressive is the temple where people are
Forced to kneel? My country is not perfect. But still

A beacon: people do not stop coming here, no
Matter the cost or pain; I imagine they see
What my mind sees; potential, the future, someplace
Where liberty is a real word; and what could be--
An atlas of happiness, showing a lamp so
Bright that hate, discord and war would sink without trace.

I speak for Connelly, Bevington, Bryant, Jones,
McHale, Ramirez, Carlo; they were leaping flames
Whose glow lights the world. Others fall to fate or chance,
But I say their souls loop the earth, their very names
A living hope, just as the acres of white crosses
Still keep watch over the coast of Belgium and France.

July-August 2011

UNDERCOVER BOSS

It's early out yet, no sign of the sun.
An alarm bell rings in a bland hotel,
And someone gets up, dresses. Their fingers
Fumble over toupees, buttons, glasses,
Possibly even a fake moustache. Then
They start out their day as a trainee,
Doing real work for once. They introduce
Themselves as Fake Name and are put to it
Right away, making dough, sorting laundry,
Carting pop around, cleaning floors, manning
The cash register, answering phones. They
Are always paired with someone who can do

Those jobs: the contrast is often striking.
By his first break, Fake Name is beat, gone, used,
Can barely move. He has not worked this hard
In twenty years. In comparison, his
Trainer is just nicely starting her twelve
Hour shift, so she can pay for braces, or school,
Dad's new wheelchair, or that trip to England
For her mom. There is normally a shot
Of Fake Name heading back to his hotel,
Totally spent, musing how anyone
Does this all day, all the time, and how they
Let it get to this. At the end, he shaves

The beard, takes out the contacts, puts away
The cardboard hat, and meets his trainers for
Real this time, as the boss. Some recognize
The voice, others are not so sure. To each
One he tells what he saw, learned, and what he
Would change. He does what he can to help with
Mom's dreamed of trip, the wheelchair, the braces, next
Year's tuition… And no matter how gauche,
Awkward, or contrived, something moving in
This, as faces thicken, and people reach for
Tissues. Many do not move or speak, their
Gratitude caught in a time before words.

They can scarcely believe what they hear, for
Until someone helps, your burden is the
Heaviest, gaining on you while you sleep.
Or it could be they are silent because
The kind words have taken them some place they
Dare not go often, a land described but
Rarely seen, where the real world was a law
So like love you could never tell it from
Your imagined, private world, where just as
You are, without one plea, you would be waves
Of light washing over an earth that held
You, the really you, for only so long.

August 2012

LETTER TO AMY ADAMS

The theatre is almost full, just past two
On Saturday. The film is close to being
Done, with most of the audience, I would say,
Mentally checked out quite awhile ago. No—
Nobody, me included, came here hoping
To think. Robin Williams (What? He must need
The work) plays TR, reduced to mere cliché;
Although he fares much better than Lincoln, who,
Of all people, spouts dull platitudes; and so
It goes--history for the folks who don't read.

So why am I here? Beauty? Undisputed;
Plus, you seem almost quaint; about your juicy
Private life, the fewer details, the better.
As usual, you're treading that line you like
To play--acting right out of *'I Love Lucy.'*
Smiling, you ask us: "Can this really be true?
Me? Amelia Earhart? She wasn't ever
Like this: didn't anyone see *'Enchanted*?'"
Even though your ear is perfect, and you strike
No false note... still, you're almost too funny, too

Over the top; but you don't wink at us, as
So many actors, even the best ones, do.
No: your Earhart is sharp, witty and smart and
About ready to be in her first big show,
You know the kind--she's sweet and true,
He means well but is a loveable poltroon,
Usually lasts thirteen weeks, then gets canned.
Since I'm watching "family" fare, the film has
To recap the story for us, nice and slow.
Now that our star's heart is bigger than the moon,

It's time he wrapped things up (quickly) with his love
Interest: he knows you, but isn't quite set
To ask you out, so they have one extra scene:
In this picture, love must conquer and amend.
He's awkward, and coughs and stumbles and stares; yet
With that quick lissome grace girls in movies have,
You teach his eyes, you are, for him, all things seen;
He takes your hand, and both of you, slowly, move
Off into that happy place where movies end;
On screen, no problem that beauty cannot save.

Yet you remain so stunning in that last scene;
Your face, light of a thousand lamps; those blue eyes,
Deeper than any ocean, an ideal match
To sky; their softness only veils their power.
The music they've picked for this shot is all sighs,
Pure yearning in A Major. Could it be we
Go to the movies for this? That funny catch
In the throat, a sign of something perfect, clean?
Found anywhere, even if it's just in our
Minds, somehow out of reach? That it's good to see

The big stars, better than us, having just too
Good a time? Their dinner for two at Cachet
Certaine... where there's never that pie-eyed loud guy
Right next to you, and the high windows all shut,
So you hear each last boring word? Don't we set
Up to fail, since the ideal can be so rare?
Amy, on the day I saw your movie, I
Was getting up my nerve to try something new,
That is, the non-ideal. It was a chance; but
For once I would be bold, for once I would dare.

Unlike your diaphanous roles, she does not
Glide from act to act, ever bright, light and fun,
A gleeful twinkle, a voice falling "as they
Say love should." Unlike you, no off screen presence
Pays her bills. Unlike you, her temper can run
Hot; not your playing kind, but a boiling lake
Of fire; when people annoy her, they should pray
That she doesn't have time to line up her shot.
She spends one-third of her time planning vengeance;
Those who charge "service" fees make a big mistake.

I used to think it was silly to reach for
What you see in the movies, where love attends
And rescues, since it can produce such friction:
Reality has a way of tempering
Our dreams, that feed on hope, with unhappy ends...
But Amy, this girl I'm telling you about
Is proof that what you have there on screen, heaven
Though it seem, is mere show, an image, a poor
Choice, when the sun lies next to me, glimmering.
And now that you and Larry are cleared of doubt,

Ready for the next sequel, this time set in
The Guggenheim, probably, what will become
Of you? Doesn't matter: nothing you have can stand.
Don't get me wrong--you are still most wonderful,
In your fashion. But I can't, now, wish for some
Thing, or idea, that's flawed in its premise,
A flimsy shanty built on the wettest sand,
Laughable lies. To pine for what you see on
Screen, no matter how bright, pure or delightful,
Means loss; a chance of a real, possible, bliss.

November 2010

NORTH MISSION ROAD

A cardboard arcade, designed by a ten
Year old--how hard can it be? Very. One
Game means rolling a big white ball into
A clearly marked blue hole; but I miss, as
Do the other (non-cheating) adults. I
Try another: this one gives you a clean
Chance, with your handful of loose change, at an
Open target. You shoot through an inch-wide
Opening with a nickel, and I miss
That too. A non-smug sign tells you an eight
Year old hit the mark one morning five times
In a row. You think ill of this child, then

Move on to something you think you can do--
Slide a marble from one end, and then to
The other, of a labyrinth made from
Cardboard, I mean, the whole damn thing's made of
Cardboard, how tough can it be, right???!!!!—still, four
Tries later, you got close, once, but no wins.
He's arranged it so that any losing
Marble shoots right back. Nonplussed, and humbled
More than you will tell anyone later,
You try the basketball game, and there, at
Last, about two-thirds of your shots go in.
The kid who set all this up has a fixed

Price: two bucks, for all day admission. He
Cheers when kids win prizes, makes no comment
With face or mouth or gesture when adults
Futilely lose time after frickin' time.
His father, off to the side, keeps an eye
On things, but with a light hand, with a just
Barely seen smile never leaving his face.
He politely answers all questions as
His son fishes out another fun pass
Or roots thru the t-shirts for a quick sale.
In the packed visitor's log, everyone
Says the same thing--"Man, I wish I was you."

They don't actually write that, of course.
They wish him well, tell him they've chipped in for
His scholarship, and "Follow Your Dreams!" and
Blah blah blah. If you ask this kid a dull
Question, like I did, he gets bored. He is
Too nice to tell me that, though, and takes my
Stupid advice (charge more for admission)
In mature silence. And suddenly I
Want sun-hot, scorching hoops of fire around
This child forever, I do more than hope
He can never age, and if he has to,
Then on his terms only. I don't doubt his

Father wants the same, that he would put up
Tall gates, and take any angels there are,
And place them outside the house he'd built, and
They'd stand by his son, and he would never
Leave, and he would never know what was near.
Because all those people coming from France
And Asia and Canada are all here
To tell him one thing. I once was you. My
World vibrated with color, every
Answer was yes, and the sky could never
Get any bluer, because I was blue sky
And a perfect June day. At Caine's Arcade

On this sunny weekend, it's a brief glimpse
At what you once were, and won't be again.
And--this time--you nod at what you read in
The homemade logbook, and think that it was
Worth the trip, in the bad taxi to a
Part of town you didn't know, to see a
Fact guessed at but never proved--age pollutes,
And time strips away wonder. And if Caine
Must age, then I hope part of him stays in
This arcade, and some sliver of him is
Always ten, never quite knowing what draws
Pilgrims to the north end of Mission Road.

January 2013

WINTER WALK

Raymond Sentes, 1943-2000. *Requiescat In Pacem.*

"The communication of the dead is tongued with fire beyond the language of the living."

(Little Gidding)

On some days I leave mid-morning for our
Day's walk: I need tea. Make that a double.
Takes awhile to get ready for our spree.
Collie #1: after a few jumps and thumps
She is set. Then a *sigh* for my trouble.
Collie #2: some wriggles and squirms and bumps
And after a short stare down, she'll allow
Me to fix her dog mantle. Collie #3…
Well, he is special. Takes less than an hour!
And then we head out west, feet crunching snow,

Into a prairie sundog. The light leaps
Out in the air like fire, the air tomb still,
Even the dogs stunned by Edmonton cold.
I walk for a break and the air and space
And the chance not to be in; the dogs will
Soon beg me to let them loose, for a race;
To them, speed is right, to go slow is theft.
Something healthy in that, the need for bold.
The urge to run fast is a faith that keeps
Its word. Leap before you look. We go left,

Walking our circle. The dogs know what comes
Next, are sure along this path or that street.
It's when they relax, knowing it's no mere
Stroll, that my dad and I talk. His shade likes
To take me for long drives in the old beat
Up piece of ---- car he said had three strikes
Against it. Most of it superficial,
Nothing, just the thoughts I need him to hear.
He laughs, and smiles out the window, both thumbs
Lightly on the wheel. For the official

"Talks," though, he pulls over, his manner stern.
The road ahead is dusty and empty,
No traffic just yet. His face chiseled wood--
Because I asked him something I should know
But don't, always. Winter is clarity:
His thinking this morning will not be slow
Or casual. He left us by permission;
Our mother said he could go rest, he should
Know we could endure. I listen, I learn,
Class is, here, now and always, in session.

> *"You ask how I know you'll be fine, since I'm not here*
> *To check on you. Like death holds me from you, cuts out*
> *Some part; as if love could be defined, like a year,*
> *Or seen on a chart. My love for you has no doubt,*
> *No measure, breadth or width, nor can it be tempered*
> *As the ocean or cooled like the seas. Stop crying. This*
> *Is not a speech. Just words from a love not severed*
> *From you, because it can't be... Your first words were bliss;*
> *Your last words lighted the darkest hours, made me free.*
> *Anyway, don't worry. My mortal eyes are closed,*
> *Perhaps for good. I wish I knew. But I still see*
> *All of you and my love for you remains transposed;*
> *It had no beginning, nor could it ever know*
> *Any end. Listen: I died, but never let go*
> *Of your hand; your soul was mine, and mine, my daughter's;*
> *There is no real death where love prays or remembers."*

This was meant to be a short walk and might
Be longer yet; the dogs don't seem to care.
Strange how the voice of the dead doesn't grow old,
Paints a different picture than what we
Would; maybe they see more than we can bear;
Or their near silence compels us to be
Still; I'll do my errands some other day.
The dogs start to get restless--they are cold,
Finally. I start us back. We take right
Homeward turns now; all of us know the way.

April 2010

ACROSS BURRARD INLET

Lucky to be even on this one. We
Almost didn't make it; our connection
Was held up by some dumb f--k skateboarding
His way down Lonsdale, peeling right in front
Of each car on the road. The bus drivers
Never pound the horn--because ignoring
Him is wise, although you would rather hunt
Him down. Stunned, we find our way to the Sea
Slug, making up a normal collection--
Starers, readers, BlackBerryers, chatters.

And I look up, and I am no longer
Young, some dull fact I may not like, but true.
No doubt there are more than a few people
Here who would consider me well past it.
I did, at their age. The signs are all there:
I have the wrong books, the wrong medieval
Clothes, the wrong phone. Time will never submit;
The gap between then and now gets stronger,
And wider. In your mind, in some ways, you
Stay a teenager, an "I" everywhere,

The whole world your stage and scene, and no need
For proof. No better age or time, and yet
What vast relief when it's over, when cold
Reality hits; freedom means you know
Youth is just an affliction to get through.
The gift of age is seeing what to hold
On to, what you are, and what to let go;
Failing that, at least you no longer read
Each random thing that happens as a set
Of personal signs meant only for you.

Is that the dock? Strange how fast this goes by;
All of us get ready to leave, even
The girl on her cell who clearly has more
On her mind. Those nearest the exits stand
Almost on alert; should we go or stay?
This journey must end, whether we loved, or
Not, or learned a great deal, or nothing, and
Wish that instead of body we were sky,
Something for a sun to rise and set in,
A broad blue canvas where pure colors play.

June 2011

RAPTURE

I used to put on the full armor of fear.
As a child it would sometimes occur to me, idly,
That after my death, life, for others, would go on. The sheer
Panic of this thought would almost make me sick,
And I'd quickly think about my new hockey stick
Or lunch or getting out of school next month.
As an adult, doubts grew upon themselves and slowly
Magnified. People talked about Love or Faith

Or Purpose and I would just dumbly stare.
What was the point--if you died anyway?
In a million years, would anyone care
What you did or didn't do? What would I aspire
To? When the earth is a ball of angry fire
No one will remember angels that are bright still
Though the brightest fell. Some would say
They find their compass in God's will,

That his law is a light… but they tend
To follow those laws as a way of sharing blame.
In church I would listen as a friend
Would tell the congregation how real, how true
The Lord was; but come Monday I knew
The decalog would be the last item in his head.
(Nor was I any better). The adults said the same
Things, but there was a wink in what they said,

Knowing everybody would get the picture.
Perhaps, like me, they were just scared.
As a child images of the rapture
Would terrify my mind. Would Jesus take
My parents and not me? What about the lake
Of fire? What about my brother?
Would everyone I knew or cared about or loved
Be gone in a flash, forever?

Or perhaps they were as bored as I was.
At bottom I'm sure they knew, or know,
That there's no heavenly father upstairs
Making sure the bus arrives on time,
Or you find that shoe. Life teaches you that, come
What may. (And it will). No matter how blurred,
People see readily enough how things really go.
To look for justice or even order in this world

Is to grope blindly in an obscure place
For an atom. Love? If it existed, mere ripples
In a vast sea, a substance that left no trace.
I sided with Iago: lust of the blood
And a permission of the will, all it boiled
Down to, and "true" love just tired shtick.
Pressed, I would say that happy couples
Had got lucky somehow, found the trick.

I'd go on to say that some need to be part of two,
I could never be half of a pair,
And of course, some of this is true
Enough: we've all seen the twosomes who speak in clipped
Tones, the double halfwits who stopped
Talking years ago, the guys (and gals)
Who always need alibis ("We're just friends, I swear"),
Their terms coy, and their 'relationship' in shambles.

Single was hardly perfect, but it beat what was out there,
A reach for anything, rather than nothing.
To me that was a shabby trade. To be... fair,
Part of me always understood, as we always do,
Since perfection is a fire we helplessly woo.
Even if we get it wrong, continually,
Still, people try for a balance--between their wishing
List picture of the world, and how that world actually

Shakes down. Some never get this right.
But most try, I believe. The old saws
Had a point; we should, since we are in someone's sight:
His aim is sure. He will never let us down; or make excuses;
Never forgets, never misses.
Death does not discern and does not care.
Rachel, I try not to paint you in salvific colors, because
The weight is too heavy, and I do not claim some rare

Insight. I hear the skeptics out there, snorting with glee.
'What--you're in love now, so no grave
For you? She redeems you, and you, she?'
No. One day, following his partially obscured map,
He will come for me and not so nicely tap
My shoulder, and show me the final obligations,
An appointment I must keep. And I'm alive
To everyone's shouted objections--

Their would haves, must bes, and ought tos.
In our own minds, we are left with what
We see, the pictures as vivid as the nightly news.
To some, I know, this will be (at best) impiety--
Others will call it dull, pointless or blasphemy.
Yet though love conquer nothing, the blend
Of love, of your shade and mine, is nothing to laugh at,
And could be the only clear way to see our end.

I was weighed down once; you are the moment when
My burden rolled away. June 19 was the seamless
Happy day that fix'd my choice, a sudden
Joy. My eyes were old once; you make them new.
Something in your eye teaches the sky to be blue;
Something in you a diapason, the soul's pure singing.
And why? Neither of us, to be fair, is flawless.
Far from it. Your faults could take up staggering

Volumes, and mine, libraries. It may sound absurd,
But truth is better out. We dissemble too easily,
A little too smooth with the written word,
And what we say often shows far too much guile.
So I ask--why? Why do you always make me smile?
Why do you lift me up thousands of miles above the ground?
What is it in you that sparks? Your leaping flame consumes me;
I once was lost, but now am found.

It's possible we were not meant to be, but
I see no harm in that. The ocean has no fate,
Has no intentions, and yet there it is, a fact,
No mere belief. The sky has no agenda: yet what we see,
The nightly star show, might as well be for you and me.
I steal from a favorite of your father's for this song;
Rachel, take my hand, Tis not too late
To seek a newer world. The night was long

Yet there are a thousand azure mornings to come;
I made many pointless journeys, but now am home;
You join me in a wavering morrice to the moon,
Our halves as one, our souls in pitch-perfect tune.

September 2009

GIANTS GAME I

A mostly packed house. That thud of a hush
When a crowd is told to be silent, lights
Everywhere around the rink, but the bright
Ones beamed on to the ice in time for the
Usual pre-game drivel. Nothing quite

Like a "nostalgia" night. The p.a. guy,
Reading his tired, overwrought script, tells us
To clap those hands together for player
A, who many of us hated, and for
Player B, who retired years before most

Of us started watching, so the applause,
When it comes, has that rote quality, a
Dutiful aspect, like crowds saluting
Dental Awareness Month. But tonight they
Have Player C, a real star in any

Heaven, and what he did on the ice still
Towers over a snowy northern game
Invented deep in the Canadian
Steppes, late on a winter afternoon. And
Those who know the sport, rightly, say he was

The best there could be. Now the applause swells
To ten times itself, waves and waves of "I
Am in the same room with history..." but
The man himself is muted, not having
An easy time of it. Dementia, who

Loses to no one, is winning this fight
Too. Our idol, in many ways the best
Ever... is partly gone. His face tells us
That. And the cheerful knowing winks, the light
Backslaps, the easy laugh we remember

From seeing him elsewhere, before, are gone.
One step in front of another is a
Challenge, and you wonder how many steps
Are left. When he finally reaches his spot,
The announcer, no longer bored, reads a

Partial list of what this man did over
Decades in a very tough game. And you
Don't want to think this but you do: which of
His Rosses, Harts, Patricks, Stanleys, would he
Trade? Would he give them all up? What about

His place in the hall? Would he skip all the
Ceremonies held in his name? Would he
Swap--for just a few more minutes? A few
More minutes before that wretched morning
When his mind clouded over, the sparks in

His mind dulled, and those great gifts, lights that made
Him an artist on two tiny blades, fled.
And if he's posed that question of any
God he cares to, by things seen it was asked
And answered, since his walk back is almost

Subdued, with less noise, the crowd now guessing
That all their real affection for this man
Will not save him from the arena with
No goals, no lights, no fans, or that second
Chance to get the last play perfectly right.

November 2012

GIANTS GAME II

Going to a game, live, always seems much
Better in retrospect; you forget that
Awful, hot packed slow bus just to get there,
Inching your way, barely grabbing the last
Seat, pricy stinky fast food, the beer stains,
Stale smoke fumes lingering near doors, a free
Gift of days when "No Smoking" was a pat
Suggestion, not the rule. And now they tee
Up every bad song you hate: It rains
Down hard and there is no escape: they blast
It all night and it reaches everywhere.
You wish they'd just play hockey, and leave such

Crap for wrestling. But (of course) the real star
Is the show, each gimmick another try
At brains without waves, people who can yell
When they are told to, and if this gives you
Pause, you can't be alone--something so sad
About mandatory, pre-ordained fun.
Strangely though, halfway through the game, the eye
Drifts lazily, slowly down to rows one
And two, by the north end, where someone's dad
Sits next to his minor league A team, who
Started dancing when they got here, and they'll
Stop when it's time to head out to the car.

Easy enough to sneer; but some sliver,
Some hidden, minute part of you, pictures
This idea: somehow these kids know best,
That the adult world, always self-aware,
Ruled by weary irony at all times,
Is just dull, and this off guard inference
Almost proved when a song you *do* like comes
On, the kids jumping up, their innocence
Keeping them, yet, from boredom or strictures,
Their joy guarded by leaping walls of fire,
The high, bright, clear bouncing tune strangely blessed,
And if only it could play forever.

November 2012

TIPS ON IMMORTALITY (AT VENICE BEACH)

Mid-winter, in this great expanse, you walk
Past huge stretches of empty lots, and still
A few spare clouds at nearly half past two.
Today the ocean gives off a faint chill,
And shoots one cold wave, and then many more,
On to fine, white sand. Over near the bike
Shop are vendors--many want to sell you
Pleasure, some hipness, some, curios, or
A crudely overpriced piece of tired schlock.
If you need to be here, you can sweet talk

Death, for the dead are all round; their fame knows
No end. Want your face on a big crappy
Clock? Don't play halftimes or be a rebel
On the morning news. Don't get fat. Don't be
On the game shows or help some old dumb cur
Win a dance contest. When the ratings spike,
Call your dealer. Don't have your own label
At Sears. Don't plug your book, with all your
Deep, as-told-to thoughts, on the late night shows:
Be against war, crime, and all the other woes.

Above all, don't be us. When they find you
In the ravine one morning, you'll still have
A star out beyond, some distant sparkling,
Something unmet, unheard, not in or of
Us, people moved always by the letter,
Never the spirit. Redeemed, you'll be like
That ocean just to your left, an inkling
And taste of infinity, and better
We never glimpse or guess at the vast blue
Depths your soul may never have traveled to.

January/February 2012

OUT FOR A WALK AFTER DINNER

Terrific Chinese food on Robson St.
Then a stroll on to Denman, where She
Treated for dessert, spoon *compris*.
The evening clement, the dusk air sweet,
We headed out to English Bay to see
Helios drift back west, leaving behind him
Oranges and reds and almost a powder blue;
Colors mixed and moved in a perfect whim,
Against the sky, in every hushed hue.

Bench #1 was fine but had too much congestion,
So to Second Beach and bench #2.
Thus my *felix culpa*, my Redeemer all too
Beautiful. To be fair, conditions for resisting temptation
Were not good. Sunset, noted. The new
Night air; see line four. Her diadem beauty:
Have a look at line thirteen. Nothing amiss.
The surf was rhythmic, powerful, in harmony,
Hypnotic. *In such a night as this...*

In such a night as this, Amanda,
We kissed, a perfect, strange rite.
I had wanted to at first sight--
And it still seemed like years. A *felix culpa?*
No, that's wrong. For one night
The muddy vesture of decay that he
So perfectly and annoyingly says is our
Fate wasn't, because of you, for me.
You make me wish a minute was an hour:

To kiss you is to be free.

July 2007, revised spring 2011

TONGUES ON FIRE

Hotter than it should be in May, the air
Just not circulating today, here, on
Sunday morning, around 11. So
When our pastor announces he's asked Jack
To turn the fans on, there is much relief.
A little later, he says "I'd like you
To stand with me, please, and sing O For A
Thousand Tongues. Number 47." It takes
A few seconds for us to stand up, look
For the hymnals, find the page and wait for

The cue. His wife, also the organist,
Flips towards the very end of her much
Bigger hymnal, nods, and we begin. Some
Of us can sing and some of us can't, but
In a group so close, who cares? We have been
Through this hymn so many times the words, though
They should shock, do not. "He breaks the power
Of cancell'd sin, he sets the prisoner free."
When we finish, before our pastor can
Even say "Please be seated," one of us

Over in the fourth row, not sitting down
Yet, begins to speak aloud, urgently,
Words tumbling, spilling out, a warning. For
Half a minute, in a message we can't
Quite make out, he tells of an upcoming
Judgement, a doom we won't escape, the weight
Of our sin is that heavy. After he
Speaks a long, strained silence. And then from a
Few rows away, someone else cannot stop
Himself: "O my people. O my people.

How you have sinned. How you have broken my
Heart. I came for you, died for you. You do
Not seek my face. You love the dark. A great,
Terrible fire is coming and you will
Not be spared. Seek my face. O my people."
No one dares to cough or find that second
Piece of gum. For all of us now, hell is
No dreamer's abstraction, but a real place
We'd chosen; and then we'd finally see
What divine and perfect justice looked like.

Did we hear a living, breathing God that
Day?--Or were we just talking to ourselves?
Was there prophecy that morning, or was
It just drama, by people who knew their
Parts? Was there a case it didn't matter?
Man has made hells Lucifer could only
Stagger at. And there are some who live in
Heaven, saved or no, since for them each day
Means another chance to serve, to help, to
Work, to bring light where before there was none.

After the service, it's much different
Out in the foyer, as we catch up on
Our news and light gossip. He who spoke in
Tongues now smiling, laughing with his friend, and
He who interpreted setting up a
Golf game for later in the week. These were
Good people I was lucky to know. So
Who was the real man? The one inside, who'd
Been set ablaze by the holy ghost, tears
Not stopping? Or the one who shook my hand

Outside, near the trees on the lot, kindly
Smiled at my inane jokes, and told me how
Gorgeous it was today, nothing better
Than halfway through spring? Could you ever get
A good empirical answer to that
Question? Each to each. Certainly it was
True that Ottawa in May felt like a
Heaven below, and staring at those skies,
You might wonder if just to be alive
Should have you forever leaping for joy.

February 2013

TUESDAY

In some ways a very normal morning:
Traffic light, but you'd never guess something
Was wrong; on TV, or in films, there are
Always 'premonitions,' hints and signs; if
Nothing else, they turn the music way up.
Today in Edmonton is late summer--
Clear sky and brisk winds. Gorgeous, actually.

But I am not surprised when the daycare
Kids get dropped off a little later than
Usual; like me, the parents were stunned
By what they saw on the news. There are looks
Exchanged, but very few words; something had
Shifted and none of us could take it in.

For what we saw on screens that morning was
Beyond chitchat. No part of us could make
Any sense: two planes into two towers;
Another into the Pentagon, then
Yet another, miles away, announcing
This: somebody had got to us, but good.

Luckily I have the kind of job that
Keeps me clear--here, like any daycare, the
Kids have one thing on their minds: whatever
Is next. To them death and bad things happen
To strangers or made up people. And this
Morning has a surreal color to it,
Like we were asleep, trapped in the wrong dream,

Hours before the alarm rings, restoring
Not clarity, exactly, but something
Which, as of now, seems long light years away:
A normal daily routine, which vanished
As fast as those firefighters ran into
The towers, saving whom they could. As if
They were sprinting into the future. And

The kids keep me busy; they can tell that
Today is strange, but I spare them the news.
Time enough for knowledge; for now, less is
More. Except one child who (I guess) had heard
Too much: "There goes my dream of seeing the
World Trade Center." I wonder--he would be

Twenty or so now. Does he visit the
Site? Does ground zero have any special
Weight? Does that day mark a time for him, the
Moment he, like every adult, knows
His immortal years are over? He grew
Up that morning and I could not check it.

And perhaps that could never be fixed. The
Parents now come, slowly, for their child. They
Are eager to see them, even more so
Than normal, but none wants to go home. And
As I hand each child back to mom or dad,
I get the same look in their eye mirrors
Have caught in mine, a plea for this to be

Monday, which now seems pastoral, the time
Before planes flew, fires raged, people huddled
Near screens gaping, as police and firemen
Rush into pillars of fire and return,
Alive or dead, holding a light in their
Hands that can never go out, since they were
Us, and we are them; and what they stood for
Is eternal.

September 2011

VALENTINE'S DAY

The sky suddenly a shocking set of
Red and pinks, splendors you only see late
In winter. Like someone is now throwing
Colors out of heaven, an artist at
Work, one without our limits, the skies as
Palette. Could a Brueghel, an Ingres, paint
On this scale? Even if this time of year
Allows only the quickest sunset, still,
It is twenty minutes of perfection
No tongue dare mimic, no brush would
Compare.

Should changelessness be what we want? People
Are always telling us to have "nature"
As our guide, but these sunsets were gorgeous
Boring eons before you or me. Worse,
They'll be pleasing others long after no
One has any idea who we are.
Should we care? Or just enjoy as is, see
If we can ignore the dull future; we
Can watch a sun fall and not bother with
The hows or whys of a very
Big star.

Is a winter sunset just that, a fact?
These baroque shades of pink remind me of
You; but does this mean anything, or is
It simply, at best, art? Something for which
Millions have no use, and… you can see
Their point. Pretty colors lift no burdens,
Save no souls. The guy assigned to clean out
Washrooms isn't expected to be thrilled
By something beautiful outside, even
If there was a window. Why would
He care?

Maybe private perfections can have no
General use--and be a total waste
Of time. Who cares? Valentine's Day might be
Pointless: and these rare sky shows outside my
Window are, anyone could say, pointless
Too. But they strike me as you strike me. As
Of things I can't fathom; like a fanfare
So vast I can't hear all of it, chords so
Wonderful they please past all reason; a
Cool breeze so fresh my soul is now
Set free.

February 2012

EL PERRERO

¿Cómo cantaremos la canción del SEÑOR en tierra extraña?

(Psalm 137:4)

We woke before the sun. The days were long,
Dusty, hot, but I didn't care. Outside
Was where the animals were, that is, where
I needed to be. Goats, chickens, wolves, dogs,
Anything not me. I could (and did) watch
For hours. My schoolroom was my grandfather's
Farm: the rest of the world could have melted
Away and I really couldn't have cared
Less. Fighting an itch, not fighting an itch,
Amounts to the same thing. I fled to my

Dreams and stayed a year in San Diego,
Becoming me, but a different me.
I loved this new country: I could not speak
The tongues of my first employers, but the
Ized Dogs I understood just fine--they wanted
Out, out, out. Until their owners hired me,
All they got was the suffocation of
Unthinking love, love that knows no bounds or
Heights. Trapped on pedestals, robbed of work or
Purpose, they bit, attacked, snarled, bared teeth, ran.

Love is free or it is nothing. But they
Were denied even that, inside all day
And all night, stuck in halls, backyards, and high
Walled dens. Love can put a hell where heaven
Would be, and these dogs were captives. In this
Place people will pay you good money to
Say the ludicrously plain; I prospered,
And moved my business to L.A; I
Am now quite wealthy. I must hire helpers
Each new year. My friends back home are happy

For me but (still) amazed. "They pay you HOW
Much to walk the dogs???" And of course it's not
Quite so simple as that. My clients here
Have strange problems--the kind that happen when
They're idle, bored, or alone. Yet the dog
Seems to care. So he or she is now turned
Into a miserable little thing,
Wearing tiny coats, or pink shoes, or signs
That say "I Love Peace." They are force-fed love
Until they puke. Then the owners are stunned

When their poor dog, with no escape, turns on
Them. You should hear the calls I get! "Fluffy
Won't eat!" "Timmy won't wear his suit!" "Chulo
Snaps at me!" Then I get there and find a
Dog who hasn't been for a walk in months.
We love cause/effect except when *we* are
The cause, the first mover. I will never
Go back to Mexico; this is home, and
The USA has heaped blessings on me,
But I wonder sometimes if we should set

Every dog free, send them to the farm
My mind visits… where dogs were just as they
Are, no one's special pet, chasing fireflies
In spring, guiding us through early fall nights,
Running after each other in the lakes,
A nimble reminder we live in a
Kind of paradise, to let the past be
The past; to never fear what could be, some
Note to yourself about life: our time here
Is mostly sweet and we have no idea.

November/December 2011

THE NATURAL NOISE OF GOOD

There are very few perfect things in life,
And even them, so briefly. Perhaps their
Brevity defines their perfection, a
Reminder of our fractured essences.
Even in music, that last place of the
Soul, the sheer ecstasy, those far heights, can

Only last for so long; at some point the
Musicians have to go home, or switch to
A song you have never really cared for,
Though you bought the album anyway. But
As the opening notes ring in your ears…
Is there, could there be, anything better,

Purer? The heart vaults over itself, too
Happy for thoughts--except of here and now.
Perhaps music is so deeply in love
With life, or love itself, that it can't stop
Shouting about joy, jumping up and down,
And singing yes, yes, yes. You click a few

Buttons, and suddenly two people you
Have never met, in the middle of a
Mostly dull song, break into a bridge that
Makes you shiver. If love calls us like this,
Then it is its own law, its own heaven,
Lightning flashes on a powerless night.

"Oh, play that thing!" It could be, should be, that
Music is love aloud. Her voice, a chord
Which gets richer yet by the hearing; her
Soul a glimmering concerto; her eye,
A blue wavering dance in the key of
C, a waltz too perfect to ever cease.

May 2011

PIED BEAUTY

Light fades in fast from the west, something
From the arctic clears out over the mountains,
Leaving green, white, crystals, fog, frost.

And there is something in the air I can't quite
Name or isolate. Life, as the poet said,
Is first boredom, then fear. Yes but

That chill in the air today feels new, not just cold,
Not just a schedule for what must happen.
You take your steps, each foot on a frozen

Sidewalk, going about your day. And he
Could have been right--for himself, and
For millions. The end is coming, he got that

Dead on. If love had a weight, would you
Feel it more in the summer or winter?
Can it survive only when the trees burst?

Or when every day is a late blue sky?
What if it happened in our heads only,
A mental event? Something to be argued

Away by the gals in the labs, and stern
Professors in last year's sweater. Or could
It inform your cold walk on the street like

Any other sidewalk, and your love like any
Other love, except that her face lights
Up an abyss, escapes any black hole,

Leaving light itself far, far behind. We might
Take a hint from maples, birch and laburnum,
Who riot in color every April whether anyone

Cares or not, for they must love their life,
Dancing in winds just in off the coast,
Swaying to a music unheard, but seen.

September/October 2012

INFATUWHATNOW?

They seem like a slew
Of impostors now, however friendly,
Light pale copies of you.

As you saw when you were here,
Light has a way of blessing the north shore.
It plays on the water, seems everywhere near,

A kind of lambent shower.
And those girls I knew were nice
And not their fault they lacked your bullying power.

I want to call them all and tell them none of it was true,
Just an image of an essence. The words, thoughts and feelings;
I may have meant them then. But then there was you.

And--to repeat--not their fault! Mostly mine, probably.
But how nice it would be to go back in time, meet you,
And--get it right, finally.

Get it perfect, in fact, a connection as deep
As cool currents in the Pacific, or
The joining of souls that must abide and keep.

If there is a God, maybe the big bang was his gamble.
Let be, and let people figure it out,
And be free, even if they fall.

Mostly they get it wrong. How could they not?
People are dumb, stupid and harsh.
But at the beginning, before there was rot--

Just air, rock and fire--and planets formed,
Maybe there was Rachel, already sun-bright and in motion,
Choiring to the cherubins, young-eyed.

Maybe those other girls, the polite
Well meaning impostors, were a purgatory;
To refine the needless, to purify my sight.

Or Rachel was a sign, a symbol of what could be,
If things were better, or not so terrible.
I wonder, sometimes, how well you see—

Your eyes in pain, forever, because of that
Awful April day. There are no words to fix or soothe;
But perhaps he can never stop smiling at what

His daughter has become--a spirit almost too rich,
Never failing, never ceasing, a polemic
And prayer for life. Because beneath the plotting bitch

Is a woman who believeth all things, endureth all things.
I bet he is happy. I hope so. Because of his daughter,
I no longer laugh at all those people who tell you what love brings.

I don't believe, but if I did,

Rachel would be an orison, a fiery star,
Or walking along the beach with her staff of fire,
Something true, no matter how far.

June 2009

STAR FLYER (for K.E.S.)

It's funny, no one envies you, though we
Should. You are about to be free of it
All; as far as you are concerned, Syria
Can go f--k itself. You can read the news
And really not care. But I bet you get

More calls than visitors, and those visits,
Brief. Folks run out of small talk fast. You don't
Mean to, but you remind us that compared
To you, we have no problems. Which of us
Looks you in the eye? Why are we quiet,

Subdued? Where's that big dramatic moment
Where we say the big, important things we
Have come to say--how much we love you, how
Much you're part of us, how much we will miss
You? Instead, it is "Stay strong," or "Get well,"

Knowing there's no chance of that. Someone has
Marked you down: you are going to a ward
More still than the one you're in now, that place
We were before birth that, although very
Dull indeed, can never be a hades

Like this hate-filled ball of mud, wind and dirt,
And people wanting or meaning to do
Good things, or telling themselves they would, but
There is this or that obstacle in the
Way and because, and because, and because.

If I see you now, on your last fair ride,
Swinging higher and higher on the Star
Flyer, circling above a city and
Its lights, and you get freer by the day,
You might, strange though it could seem, be the most

Happy, and wish us the same state, and there
Would be no tears, since you'd wiped them away,
Laughing too hard from thirty-eight great years,
And you had learned that this weird blue ball can
Still be, wherever there is love, perfect.

July 2012

HEAVEN

Always so *dull* up there. The craziest
Film, TV show or novel brings us the
Same thing, over and over--big, puffy
White clouds, angels hovering, golden lights,
Bland serenity. And our bright ideas,
Bold as we say they are, stop right about
There. Something in us that cannot handle
Happy, can't sketch it out. Even the strong
Poets, the ones who could do anything,
Are struck quite dumb here. Dante is nowhere

Duller than Paradise; and even Donne
Is reduced to singing along in a
Hymn with no end. Did that clever Spanish
Dreamer have it right--that heaven, for most
Of us, is just this life, minus what can't
Be helped? I'd be me, and you'd be you, but
No more bills, no more being put on "hold,"
And everything free at the store… and time
Would heal what our minds can't. Or won't; maybe
Mortality was just a sketch for sin,

A rough draft, at best, and eternity
Would teach us to be still. Love would tag-team
With Time to beat up his old foe, Hate. Yet
I wonder who would win that match--like me,
My friends are as they once were, just older;
Learning seems to be something others do
While we rehearse our mistakes, polishing
Some sins into never-meant-tos; and though
The wages might be Death, who has yet to
Meet hundreds who are just waiting him out?

Heaven is that last, late, unlooked for guest, some
Bright mystery, something best not found, some
Ball thudding into a glove, right by the
Sea, some vision, someone just for you, with
Your hand in theirs, underneath whispering,
Sibilant trees, some love unspeakable,
Some joy out of nowhere, something bubbling,
Spilling out of your soul, a rhapsody
In any color, some pink orange red
Setting sun, even if the night will come.

December 2011

CLEAR GLASS

It is one of those perfect days TV
Commercials are filmed in; endless blue skies,
Leafy trees, grinning families, new hopes
Without end, as the SUV glides off
Into serene eternity. And for
Whatever strange reason, I can't help but
Think, as I sit there on the perfect log
On the perfect beach, watching the perfect
Waves roll in, of the idiot rapture
Predicted by yet another Bible-

Toting reverend. It (the Rapture) did
Not come today, as I'm sure he knew it
Would not. So long as the checks clear, why would
He mind about the end? His, mine, yours? But
He sits and thinks and stews, and reads and re-
Reads, and pronounces this day the chosen
Scriptural hour, The End Of All Time. So
Over the next few days he will blame the
Signs and mysteries, prophecies that led
Him astray. He will want to add up those

Numbers, take a harder look at Daniel.
Maybe with enough study he will come
Up with another date--and again the
Media will pretend to care. And yet...
We know not to. He ain't coming. Some part
Of us, though, needs a big movie ending,
Where lights flash, good people are rewarded,
Judgements are handed down, the fires of hell
Stoked, those whom we hate burning, burning. And
Everything right now, as we dream things

Should be, and above all, everyone
We love alive forever; a place no
Age can stale, no circumstance can alter.
That is what the rapture fuss is about--
Love. And someone wiping away all tears,
Not needing those anymore, since death can
Never again separate. That greasy
Fraud fills his bank account with our fears; knows
We all want to be where there is no more
Pain, or sorrow; where death has passed away.

Or perhaps he is no thief, merely a
Believer in certain things happening
For reasons beyond us. Or he thinks that
A just god can only abide so much,
That someday he will come to purify.
But what if there is no final tableau?
My perfect girlfriend, sitting on the same
Perfect log on the perfect beach, laughs, and
Tells me about her day. She, for one, is
Not waiting for end times, codes and wonders.

Instead she takes my hand for a walk on
The seawall, ocean to our right, gardens
And houses to the left. She points to a
Heron swooping, stars coated milky blue.
Nods when I say I love her, laughs again,
Takes my hand more firmly. This is better
Than a Revelation. And on our way
Home finds blue flowers among the gardens,
Brighter still after a long rain-drenched night,
Brighter still among a rich, luscious green.

June 2011

CHRISTMAS LIGHTS
For R.A.S.

Δόξα ἐν ὑψίστοις θεῷ καὶ ἐπὶ γῆς εἰρήνη ἐν ἀνθρώποις εὐδοκίας.
("Glory to God in the highest, and on earth peace, good will toward men.")
Luke 2:14

I

The cars race along like they're at a track meet,
Everyone in a hurry. Six o'clock. People speed
Right past you, unseeing. Just like last year...
They forgot. And now have a million things to do.
Evening rain falls on their heads, reflected in street
And car lights. *"What about something for that guy*
At work? I think he said a hamper. What about my
Mother? Right, she said flowers. Dad? A mere
Grunt, said 'Anything would be fine indeed.'
Cards for relatives I don't see. Uhm, something new

For my 'special' someone. Her hints are oblique..."
Something like this through every head,
Even the ones so far from God they don't mean
To even pretend to care. How could He
Matter? The 'merely' secular has no room for mystique.
So why the fuss? Especially all those tacky signs.
Why the shopping and the hustle and the lines
And the sighs at the cash machine?
("I should have gone to Wal-Mart instead.")
And why, above all why, the sudden charity?

II

Anchors who sternly tell you about Unrest In
Pakistan pause, blink once or twice emotionally,
And then earnestly wish you the best of the season;
Stores play song after song celebrating the redeemer--
A man who would shut their business down within
Seconds. Even the beer companies get profound,
The tone subdued, ancient hymns thundering in the background.
In car ads, very briefly, the shilling stops for some reason,
As the couldn't-be-happier mixed race family
Stares and grins at the brand new Beemer.

And goodwill towards whom? Christmas,
Just like poetry, makes nothing happen.
We can sing carols all we want, and never cease,
But the men in caves will keep planning our death;
Nor does it end hate or bring even fleeting justice
To the near, far or middle east. Fear and war always prevailing
Over the child born in Palestine, his parents fleeing
Caesar. His beginning did not bring peace,
Nor did his end. We read that he was forsaken,
Asking the unanswerable with his last breath.

III

Still, even the atheist and agnostic treasure this time,
Their trees, like the devout, a spire of hope.
Something in the season grips us, despite
The shouting ads and clanging clichés, reindeer
And a little drummer who triumphs in rhyme,
Or Mommy kissing Santa Claus at half past two.
On that late December night, the frost reaches you,
As your breath blooms clouds, almost white,
A clear full moon reflects on the steep slope
Of snowy streets. It stops you, the frozen sheer

Beauty. You turn the corner, and someone has dazzled
Their tall cedar; the blinking lights a symphony,
Sparkling, little bubbles of rhapsody, tiny stars,
Reminders of a love so perfect no hatred could destroy.
Rachel, you are a bliss slow unfurled;
You make the old new, and the new, bright;
You were there in the beginning, daily my delight.
I hear her, in the north, singing to the auroras,
Her soul an aria, fanfare and harmony,
As she repeats a sounding joy.

December 2009

THE OLD RUGGED CROSS

David, they have spent a long afternoon
Talking about you. Some mourners have tried
Wry stories, one or two have tried wistful,
Some have tried humor, some, the Bible, some
Have let their sheeting tears speak. People wind
In and out of anecdotes, searching for
Something to say that isn't a version
Of *'I can't take this,' 'This sucks,'* or *'Why? Why?'*

Because, believer or not, they know you
Ain't coming through that door, with the duct tape
On your shoes, the crazy costumes, a kid
Alive and in love with life's puzzling fun--
Its crucial, essential absurdity.
Believers hope to see you again, in
Another manner; those without hope cling
To the times your spirit was joy diffused.

And David, I need not tell you that what
They might say, however fond or rueful,
Changes nothing. When they are done speaking,
Words cease to matter. Again. They take your
Body out of the church, your friends have a
Firm grip; they will not let you falter. They
Stare at the ground; anything but think of
Where you are going, what they are doing.

In other lives lost, we have (some) comfort.
When their end comes--"Nothing is here for tears."
He had his time, good and bad and the dull
In between. He had his kick at the can--
And believe me, some people kick it good--
All of us almost resigned to that fate…
Whereas you hadn't escaped high school yet,
The eye's dungeon, and the brain's dark prison.

You will not know how good it is to be
Free of all that. You never had the chance
To read your instruments, prepare for flight,
Destinations unchecked, paradise found.
A few speakers in the house of the Lord,
In desperate search for peace, spoke of God's
True plan. It must be an odd plan, the kind
That shoots down misery, sickness and death

In a hailstorm just now gathering strength.
That deep sorrow is forever you now
Unwillingly prove. When your friends take you
Outside, your brother, on the far right, helps
Lift the casket. Behind him, a few small
Awful steps, your mother and sister strain
Just to stand. As bad as your service was,
The promise of life cut brutally short,

This is worse--your father's face. It is wracked
And tortured and bewildered and so pained
It beggars these lines. Like he can know no
Further outrage, no more grief. And in his
Hand, a slim white cross, which, tiny as it
Is, he can barely hold. What kind of 'plan'
Would ever encompass this ache? What could
Encircle it with healing, make it whole?

Perhaps he hopes to see you again, and
For his sake, I hope he's right. Perhaps as
You took your leave late that May evening,
Soaring over Ottawa and its clean,
Wide streets, you took a moment to hold your
Father up, as he stared at perfect blue
Skies; perfect because you once played under
Them; and still beautiful, though robbed of you.

July 2010

NOVEMBER 7, 2008
(FOR ILSA SUSANNAH LANGLOIS HAGERMAN)

I

Even the childless celebrate a new
Birth. It is weird, our love for beginnings.
Adults foolishly say 'Happy New Year,'
As if this year will be any better
Than last year's crapfest. Our troubles still mount.
The past's holocausts are never the last
Word. There is always some group of halfwits
Resolved to somehow 'purify' their land,
Always some guy going to walk into
A store, anywhere, and start shooting. There's
Never any shortage of evil and
What it lives on. When we say that something
Is "just human nature," it's never a
Compliment. Just a shrug at what won't change.

II

Ilsa, why are we so happy about
You? It's not just that you are lucky, born
To parents who will love you past the end
Of all infinities. Within three days
Your mother said you were the very best.
And it's not just that you are twice lucky,
Born into a culture of ease. Riches
Are a mixed blessing: there was no need to
'Diet' for our wretched and bad tempered
Ancestors; no earnest highbrow talk shows
("Whither Western Europe?"). In fact, if we
Do have a problem, it's having too much,
All the time… even in your mother's spare,
Sparkling bright clean, ecumenical house.

III

And it's not just that you were smart enough
To be born a girl; you will live longer,
Be able to tell a man just about
Anything--and get away with it, and
Never have to make the first move. Bonus:
No one, ever, will expect you to have
Any idea what might be in your purse.
Instead, our happiness and hope in you
Is rooted in something else. To the world,
A child is a promise: since things could be
Good, they will be. We live on, most of us,
Even if we constantly tell ourselves
And our friends that we want out. We don't mean
It; our sheer happiness in you is proof.

IV

Ilsa, I ask again; why is it you
Make us so happy? Your arrival here
Is an announcement--what is might not be.
Perhaps a child is a fresh start, a chance
To begin anew. So I hope that by
The time you might read this, these words will be
Embarrassingly dated. I hope the
Death camps will have closed. For good this time. And
I hope the men who opened those camps are
Stacked high, wide and deep in the ninth circle.
I hope you will not read stories about
'A man who seemed perfectly normal, when--'
Or 'a woman who never meant to hurt--
But.' Let hope be a fire in the long night.

V

I am tempted to end this with lists, of
Dos and don'ts, that is, because your journey
Begins now. Like us, someday you will have
Your share of flaws. There will be days when you
Wish everyone in the Milky Way would
Just *shut up*. And that's ok, and you don't need
Good advice. (Nor would you take it. No one
Does. Our little secret). Instead, let me
Close with a confession: I lied to you
Earlier about what your mother said;
Listen; this is what she actually wrote;
Rhapsodic, she called you a 'vision of
Perfection,' and she was right to say so;
Because of what you are, what you may be.

November 2008

PERFECTION ON EARTH

It could not be dark just yet, here in mid-
Town, at around eight, on this summer's night.
We walked east on Wilshire, past Fairfax, and
Checked out the LACMA shops and exhibits--

Or rather, you were, for I (to be frank)
Was furiously searching through my shirt
Pocket for "It," the big surprise, the main
Reason I brought you here, a ring that would

Stand in for whole, matchless, bliss. And--in a
Stroke of luck for me--at eight, right on time,
They flicked some kind of switch: Chris Burden's strange,
Odd, beautiful art was lit, all over,

Like happiness beyond lips, eyes, and ears.
Those lampposts, which must have cost him hours, weeks,
And long years, and which he placed not quite in
Rows, now stood in attendance. And if you'd

Been there, in a light movie rain, under
A half-black, half-blue sky, scattered around
A few people who did not care, you might
Have seen something falling out of the dusk,

Something amazing, something rare--perfect,
Real freedom. A man, down on a knee, showed
A woman a light powder blue box, and
When she closed the ring around a finger,

The sky opened up heaven, the mountains
Shouted until morning, and if there were
Any burdens, before, then now they rolled
Fast away. Here is a mystery: love

Cannot outlast you or me. An essence
This pure can never stop sounding joy, a
A soprano forever pealing high,
Happy melismata, and will not know

Death, and even he might ask us to stay
Our infinite dance, to teach the earthbound
About love, so wonderfully made, and
The one escape from limits, time and chance.

January 2013

AT FLYBALL

The building is tough to find and
Out of the way. The entrance is
Not marked, but you end up choosing
The door on the left. Funny how
When people want to come, you don't
Need signs. We walk through the lobby
Of a curling club, a few folks
Eating lunch and reading the news,

Then to the floor, where you'd expect
Ice, but now is set out in halves--
One side for rest, one for games. We
Stroll past the Puget Hounds, the Free
Fur Alls, the Dream Team, the Muttniks,
All waiting their turn. Around them
Owners shoot the breeze and make snacks,
As if they don't hear the googol

Of barks, each one louder than the
Next; it is racing day. The Hounds
And Muttniks are not here idly;
Their chance is coming. Intrigued, we
Wander over to see the eighth
Race, two teams barely able to
Wait. Lights go all the way up to
Red, then two yellows, then, at last,

Green. By which point two dogs burst past
Us, blurring, too fast for words. "Flight"
Meagrely, poorly, describes their
Launch into the air, since they go
Over hurdles like humans go
Over ants. They leap into a
Box that gives them a ball, then turn
Around, for a sprint back even

Faster. Before they are all the
Way back, two more fly right by them,
Running the same course; two more from
Each team will do it, and then the
Shortest time wins. Some of the more
Gifted dogs minuet their way
Through the runs, paws barely touching
The track, as if they raced flyball

At birth. I ask around. Some are
Naturals, setting new records
Since they were one or two. Others
Grow into it, steady members
Of a team. Others don't care; they
Play catch with the ball, or ignore
Hurdles, or run in the wrong lane.
Rachel says: "I once saw a dog

Sit down in the middle of a
Race." She laughs at the memory.
Apparently the mutt was bored,
Or the game had ceased to matter.
"What do the teams get if they win?"
"Nothing," she laughs again, fondly,
"Just bragging rights, mostly." "So why
All the..." I decide not to ask.

"Because we're crazy," she answers,
Chuckling again. She might be right.
Outside I see vans from the whole
Northwest, quite obvious the sport
Is a major part of life for
Hundreds, thousands. And all this for
Races with no prize at the end. Some
Dogs snag a Milkbone here and there,

But other than that, the only
Reward is flight, and I am not
Sure whose heart soars more, ours, watching
Pure speed do what it is here for,
Not earthbound like we are, or theirs,
Finally freed from their owners'
Gentle hands, told to 'Go get 'em,'
And off they go after a ball

Like every ball, and finishing
By chewing on a common rope.
Strange: but maybe these odd flyball
People, with their charts, vertical
Scoring rules, and by-law panels,
Are onto something; art is a
Place marked with no main entrance. Though
I guess the sport was invented

By a man with a lot of high
Energy dogs, the sport is no
Different than what some of us
Get up to. And it's better to
Try for a race exactly right,
The best time ever, than attempt
Nothing, do nothing. Coming up
To noon, there's a lunch break, so we

Decide it's time to go, and start
Our goodbyes. Rachel would linger,
Not sure she wants to leave what held
Her so long--such a clear picture
Of bliss, dogs sprinting at glorious
Speed, 'for what must be joy,' barking
At the end, every time, to say
The truth--"I won, I won, I won."

June 2011

SNOW AT NIGHT

I can't believe I'm saying this to you, Amanda,
Because I used to hate it.
Snow at night was an enigma.

And not the good kind: it meant
(At the very least) lots of
Shoveling, sometimes an all morning event,

While my dad watched.
(He liked it done a certain way).
And if the snow had really piled

Up, enough to (*dies mirabilis!!!*) cancel the buses,
Well, my parents usually managed
To chauffeur my brother and I in to school regardless.

And it gave my paper route a hellish shape.
("Is there enough snow for ya eh?")
I vowed one day to move, to escape.

Now I live in a city where, since people
Don't have to deal with slush all year,
They (quite rightly) think of snow as magical.

When it does come here, I have seen
Them stop--especially if they are at work--
And stare, stunned by a sky suddenly serene.

Because it seems like a blessing by sight;
The way snow at night brings its holy hush,
The old familiar now a new sparkling white.

Les neiges d'antan might be gone, for good,
But who cares? Those tiny little soft kisses
From up high tell us of other things. If we would.

Amanda, *comme lys*, in her splendid array,
Could help me look at night, and--if she can abide the cigar smoke--
Through Eden make our solitary way.

December 2008

NICOLE ON VACATION

Only a complete and total dick
Loves camping. I mean, get real.
Let's get back to nature, and "rough" it,
But on our terms, *s'il me plait*.
But I am a crazy chick,
And thus I have driven some way
And arrived here in Berwick.

Playing cards in the rain.
Wondering about mildew levels in tents.
Swatting flies. No shortage of them, in summer,
In Nova Scotia.

Because of weather, my housework roster
Has been sharply curtailed. I only get
To wash the dishes twice a day. I was forced
To leave my vacuum at home.
I have to admit Keith's children snicker
When they see their *bellemere*, in the gloom,
Pinesoling the camper.

But I keep my spirits up! I am Nicole;
Gloom is not in me. It can't rain all week,
Even in the Maritimes. If it does,
Things could be worse.

That is, the rains--eventually--will rescind.
And I am here with my family at work and play.
Unlike others I could name--pining
For what he isn't sure he wants. And should he try?
I thought of him yesterday, as the light dimmed;
Outside the tent, hushed wings flew by.
I could hear him in the wind.

The Haida tell us a raven once stole the light of the world.
And for that, and his other sins,
He is "doomed to continue
Forever his restless wanderings."

Some might characterize his fate as sad.
I don't know. Our lives are brief: some of us
Redeem this with love, or a bond
That, when spoken, is true.
And some cling to a love they wish they had.
Others, seeing what those bonds can do,
Think the raven doesn't have it so bad.

August 2008

NIGHT STORM

That you would not die, would be best.
Frankly, I just can't picture it,
Even as some weird theory.
I see stories in the papers,
And on TV; they trouble me.

A hiker gets lost in the woods.
A train runs awry, killing eight.
A big car pileup leaves six hurt,
Four grievously. The hospital
Can't identify and can't cure

The new virus; story at ten.
My point? This could be you or me.
And then what? Would you build a pyre
For me? And then? Would I set a
Memorial in stone for you?

Would people be stunned by our wit?
Our guess--that someday it would end?
They might grin at my sly Greek text;
My friends would love your ironic
Friendly digs at your jerk boyfriend.

O that Rachel was not mortal,
That love, or these lines, redeemed me,
And had you breathing forever.
Shakespeare is still outside of time,
Yet no one who he loved is here.

I walk home in the electric
Storm, my skin crackling. The sky booms
And shakes; the night winds a prelude
To angry thunder; lightning streaks
Across clouds, the wet streets sizzling,

As if Rachel, as metaphor,
Is now complete, since if she is
Not eternal, then the evening's
Northern lights prove our love fast; and
Flecks of summer rain prove it true.

September 2010

THOUGHT EXPERIMENTS

Non posse non peccare.
(Augustine, *The Confessions*)

Timeless mother,
How is it that your aspic nipples
For once vent honey?

The pine-tree sweetens my body.
The white iris beautifies me.
(Stevens, *In the Carolinas*)

I

Do you ever wonder, Amanda, even this late,
About ifs? If we (for instance) had a more typical tale?
And do you ever wonder about whys?--
That is, why you and me? Neither of us qualifies as a tease;
No friends would ever suggest us for *Blind Date*;
Nobody would dream of calling us "normal."
That's mostly ok with me, since couples run the full scale.
Some seem deliriously happy, some in a silence now long habitual;
A few in the middle range, quietly at ease,
Choosing what they know over infernal lows, singular highs.

II

Last night I had dinner with someone
Who, for all his many virtues, is not you.
I bring this up only to ask: Was this our goal?
Did we know? That it wouldn't work, I mean.
In Ottawa I often paid you a great deal of attention.
Sometimes you would flatter, and sometimes mock.
Life is mainly dull. And pointless, too.
But your touch was electricity incorporate; I still remember the shock.
Before, just dullness, and now a light seen;
Your voice to me an annunciation, the just made perfect. And whole.

III

In the terrace of Il Giardino I sat and wondered.
Why I am here on business? Shouldn't I be
Pouring you a second glass of the third cheapest wine?
(God save you from a man known for frugality as sacred writ).
Possibly it's because we're better at happiness deferred--
Short sublime instead of daily problems that somehow double.
Probably, it was good for you to be in Japan, and me in B.C.;
We are by no means a perfect couple.
Plus there was "The Weakness." Plus I could be a haughty shit;
You were right, I think, to see our problems as mine.

IV

Not that I intend to take all the blame!
Far from it. Back then, we had yet to learn the art
Of agreeing to differ. Your body was beauty, captivated;
I wasn't alone in noticing your lineaments of grace.
We had something between us we didn't care to name--
(The haughtiness was just part of the difficulty).
Possibly it's because our divided halves had, from the start,
Faults our whole cannot heal. Possibly
Aristophanes should have gone on to trace
The dances of halves enchanted.

V

Whatever happened, I want to tell you
How you make me feel--if only by bad rhyming.
You are those moments in Mozart when he is a holy fire.
You are a clear morning after months of drizzle,
A world made new.
If we lived in Paris, it would always be June,
You would be the Seine lit up in the evening,
Our almost affirmations made under the gibbous moon;
The slow, passing boats as a votive candle,
Reveling in the night air.

VI

Possibly the cherry tree shakes out its blossoms
As an evening compline, a supplication
For something perfect and true.
Maybe my answer is this: there can be
No if or why here, only an is.
I hold your hand in the dusky light
For the same reason Orion
Has its slow east-west march at night;
For the same reason you like me,
And the fall sky a deep blue.

October 2008

SING-ALONG-MESSIAH

You, sir, are stuck at some unspeakable
Sing-Along-Messiah. You have sat there
Many minutes, while the moron in front
Of you pretends to be "Gee-org" Handel,
Disgruntled composer. You're not alone:

The contralto is pretending he's not
There; to your far left is the guy handling
The bass; gorgeous chick on your right, is, I
Guess, going to handle the soprano;
Might be good--I don't plan to be around.

The inane shtick goes on awhile, a bad
Actor doing his high culture routine.
Pleased, the audience laughs and laughs, chuckles
On cue. The gag is that God has made a
Deal with Handel--immortality, so

Long as there's a sing-along-Messiah
Each year. He says: "It was an offer I
Couldn't refuse." The audience laps this
Up too. Leaning lightly on the cane he
Has to remind us that Handel is old,

He shuffles over to the conductor's
Rostrum, where he sits with a huge thump. "Now,
If we're ready, let's begin," he intones.
He lifts the baton with a flourish: and
The orchestra plays the overture, done

In a little under three minutes. Then
A hush beyond silence, as you start your
Word painting, your voice commanding the hall:
"Comfort ye, my people." By the time you
Have sung that her warfare is accomplished,

I, for one, can't take anymore, again
Undone by this music. There are no words
For these raptures; you are the only sound,
The symphony very quiet. Why isn't
Life like your powerful voice, your perfect

Grasp of tone, melody, pitch? You make me
Happier than I can speak or tell. On
Your face the faintest of smiles, as if you
Can't quite believe your luck, being able
To sing so flawlessly the perfect words,

Bright peals, matched to heaven. "Prepare ye the
Way of the Lord; make straight in the desert
A highway for our God." I am still in
Tears, and I am by no means alone; the
Panning cameras show more than a few

Misty faces. Handel has you gliding
And soaring high, finally, triumphing.
As you come to the end of the verse, "and
The rough places plain," your face, I'm sure you
Can't help it, now is a smile, all alight.

How do you do this? How can notes scribbled
On a page years ago make us shiver?
Contrary to the old hack's tired act, his
Art did not save Handel; and whoever
Wrote Isaiah's words has long been dead too.

Yet on stage tonight both men, prophet and
Musician, are fiercely alive, ablaze;
Death has no dominion over these souls:
They have no bounds, their magic cannot be
Darkened or dulled. No tyrant can touch it.

Perhaps you smile since you are too happy,
And your voice can no longer contain it,
A spirit speaking. Lacking answers, I
Simply rejoice greatly in what music
Is: hope in even the very darkest

Hour. We live in times that might stagger a
Dante, would leave an Isaiah without
Speech; yet the prophet said "Comfort ye," and
A man in Dublin brought perfection to
Us, his arias a far-off fire in

A deep night. Perhaps I presume falsely.
That evil lives and breathes and prospers is
Not really in doubt. But while the tenor
Shouts with joy, there can be a real belief:
That our yoke is easy, our burden, light.

December 2010

AMBLESIDE

Just after three... I should be working. But why should I?
Instead I am dazzled by you, quite unfurled.
So I will take a moment or two from my day
And feebly try to paint la Sentes, by my eye.

Late light, far in the west; once a blaze, now a soft ember.
That time a few moments before the end
Of the fireworks, where the designer shows off,
The sky alight with shocking-happy blue, red, amber.

Or at evening, when the heat begins to fade,
And in the day you have reveled,
Happy just to be--and there comes along
That perfect breeze, like mercy new made.

Brief glimpses of our mastery,
Of something reached for, and gained,
When you move with ease what you used to strain at;
The soul at home with its compound mystery.

Neruda: "Laughter is the language of the soul."
True, because you complete the jokes in my mind;
A match of time and spirit, of contrapuntal harmony,
The divided half mended and whole.

Your hand there as I reach for it, Rachel,
And your head the ideal fit for my shoulder; lend
Me your beauty; let me be your bed,
All of your body my cradle.

As darkness falls, and we are caressed by slow lovely
Zephyrs, I need you to take up my hand
For our stroll along Ambleside;
The holy hush of the evening sea

Calls us; we take our pew along the beach; our day is ending.
Since we are one, our hymns are entwined;
Even if this all in my head, our private service
Can have no better setting,

Since perfection is here and forever, and you are my eyes, gleaming.

July 2009

ENGLISH BAY

May, with its light behaving
Stirs vessel, eye and limb,
And reminds me of Amanda.

Yesterday I thought: "There is no system.
I was miserable this morning,
My mood an obnoxious thunder,
Unusually crapulent, even for me--
I hated everyone and everything.
But I sit here in English Bay, stunned
By an almost embarrassing beauty;
If Amanda was here, I would be perfect.

Anywhere she is is Eden.
She is a dance of cherry blossoms, rain washed,
Playing in ecstatic blue splendor."

May 2008

WHOSE HEART IS CONQUERED

Late autumn in Mundy Park, just before
Christmas, there are much fewer of us than
Usual. Though summer would find hundreds
Of walkers and sprinting dogs, today there
Are a mere handful, the walkers pausing
To blow noses and tighten hats and scarves.
You can see why most would stay away. In
July this leafy park is one thing, in

December, quite another. What in light
Seems like Eden is, today, a glimpse of
Age--and then the only end of age. Crisp
Breezes chill you right through, what sun there is
Feels pointless. It warms nothing and will soon
Set anyway. Some trees that in June thronged
And burst now are uprooted because of
Last night's windstorm. Years and years of life, all

Over. The stump of one is bigger than
Five of us together. Not even the
Dogs want too close a look; in fact, one kind
Of hides behind me--no fool, she can hear
All too clearly what this tree preaches: "It's
Coming one day, my friend, it's coming. I
Was here for hundreds of years. I thrived. All
Who wanted shade found it underneath me.

I was food for some, a house for others,
A stopping place for still more. And one strong
Wind and I was gone." The winter solstice
Is so close there will be no escaping
That sermon, listening or not. Strange to
Think these thoughts near Christmas, with a fall snow
Drifting over dark woods, each flake too light
To really settle anywhere. At this

Time of year you think about love, if it
Has any force, if it survives us, if
That child in a manger really could mean
Salvation. Do we want it to be true?
Some are so evil I don't want to hear
Of a pardon. Could that boy have been a
God, immortal? Could he bring peace? To ask
That is to know our limits. The tree shows

Us, argue all we might, that nothing here
Need be; someday, something so pure and good
And helpful will get the push. And us? Not
Always so good or pure or helpful; not
Everyone will mourn our end. Too dark
For further walks into the park, we now
Find our way out, the snow a little more
Driven, blown by a harder wind. We look

Down, our footing less sure. One of the dogs,
Skittish all day, suddenly right by me,
None too thrilled that she can't see clearly and
Can't identify all the scents of dusk.
Just after four, near Foster Avenue,
We take a right, since that's where the car is.
You say: "Can anyone see?" I say "No."
"Good. Give me a sec." She takes her strong-willed

Dog, the big one with the muzzle and the
Shortest leash, out into the field of a
Baseball diamond. (Sadly, his bark is not
Worse than his bite: the leash is short for a
Reason and the muzzle is not some cute
Affectation). The other two dogs go
With you, not wanting to miss anything.
When you're far enough away from the path,

You quickly unleash him and take off his
Muzzle and invent a few games for him,
Which delight him past care. He cannot stop
Smiling or laughing. The other dogs take
His new freedom the way they always do;
One tries to play along, but is baffled.
The other strolls over to see me, and
Asks if it's time to go. I nod. She nods.

She does not know what is next, continues
With her sort-of-herding, ambling to you
And back. Now your smiles nearly equal his;
The strong-willed dog has, again, multiplied
Your love, stunned as always by your hail of
Blessings. Death has no law over this love;
His leaping in the air reminds us of
Something true: whose heart is conquered is saved.

December 2010

JOY UNSPEAKABLE
(FOR NELL LUCIENNE LANGLOIS HAGERMAN)

I was so pleased to hear about you, Nell.
That you're here is the best news possible.
Bright April of this year sounded the bell
Of complete joy; nothing comparable
To your inexpressible perfection.
Each day a fresh lesson; you gently teach
To keep praising; happy is an action.
Life's a gift. What we do with this, what reach
We have, is up to us, but you remind
Us our delight in this world must not cease;
Be, for our sake, the gift of tongues refined;
A soul can wander, and yet be at peace,
Man may fall, but I hope Nell never will,
She is bliss, even if there is hell still.

June 2010

POETRY IN TRANSIT

Always free verse; always first person singular.
Speaker is either a chick whose dead mom
Liked apples (crunchy ones), or a dreary shit
Who loves his partner. Or the lines are about
Nature--shiny pebble in a quiet brook; a dog barks;
The way tides go in and out;
Soulful walks in picturesque parks.
Reading just one Poem in Transit
Has you checking out the ad for Imodium
Or perusing the back of your transfer.

Strange, since it's a beautiful idea; the long crawl
On Marine Drive allows you plenty of time
To read; sure would cut down on the stress.
That surly wordless driver and his rocking,
Back-wrenching brakes. Eight stops from the mall,
You hear all the cell phone yelling: "Yeah, I'm
On the bus!!!" And the vague urine rank;
The ad above you about Not Smoking;
Nothing so slug-like as the 239 Express,
Slower than the queue at a "full service" bank.

Poets who are any good would grab you, shake you,
Make you forget your missed connection.
Although the poets next to the ads may be new,
They're up there because they're local,
Or someone in Victoria handed out money;
Never any great art when the "people" pay.
If we all take the bus and at least fake being social,
Putting up with crowds, rain and congestion,
Then let the poems above our heads shower euphony,
Let words heal the scars of a long day.

September 2000, revised spring 2011

About the Author

Brian Wood was born in 1970 and attended the University of Ottawa and the University of Toronto, receiving a Master's degree in English in 1994 after putting his professors through hell. After graduating he moved to Vancouver where he worked for Coles and then Indigo. In 2006, he became a literary agent, representing such people as Bob McKenzie, Al Strachan, Brian Kilrea, and James Duthie. He enjoys watching NFL games on TV, reading, writing, playing tennis, and listening to music, in roughly that order.

His website is www.brianjwood.com.

www.ingramcontent.com/pod-product-compliance
Lightning Source LLC
Chambersburg PA
CBHW071513040426
42444CB00008B/1631